THE BOOK OF THE ANIMALS™

EPISODE 1

Bilingual English-French

When the animals don't want to wash.

Quand les animaux ne veulent pas se laver.

Frog didn't want to wash his feet.
He said, "No, no, no… I don't want to wash my feet! No way, no!"

"They say that when you don't wash your feet, it smells really, really bad!" a smiling Cow said.

<table>
<tr><td>QUIZ</td><td>HOW DO YOU SAY:</td></tr>
<tr><td colspan="2">frog, want, wash, feet, no way, smells, bad, cow</td></tr>
</table>

La grenouille ne voulait pas laver ses pieds et dit : « Non, non, non… Je ne veux pas laver mes pieds. Pas question ! »

« On dit que quand on ne se lave pas les pieds, ça sent très, très mauvais ! » lui dit une vache souriante.

Cow didn't want to wash her hair.
She said, "No, no, no… I don't want to wash my hair. No way, no!"

"They say that when you don't wash your hair, it itches and itches and itches, all the time!" a laughing Bird said.

QUIZ	HOW DO YOU SAY:
	hair, itches, all the time, bird

La vache ne voulait pas laver ses cheveux. Elle dit : « Non, non, non… Je ne veux pas laver mes cheveux. Pas question ! »

« On dit que quand on ne se lave pas les cheveux, ça gratte, gratte, gratte tout le temps ! » lui dit l'oiseau en riant.

Bird didn't want to wash his eyes.
He said, "No, no, no… I don't want to wash my eyes. No way, no!"

"They say that when you don't wash your eyes, you can't see the lovely blue sky anymore!" a smiley Fox said.

<table>
<tr><td>QUIZ</td><td>HOW DO YOU SAY:</td></tr>
<tr><td colspan="2">eyes, see, blue, sky, fox</td></tr>
</table>

L'oiseau ne voulait pas laver ses yeux.
Il dit : « Non, non, non… Je ne veux pas laver mes yeux. Pas question ! »

« On dit que quand on ne se lave pas les yeux, on ne voit plus le joli ciel bleu ! » lui dit une souriante renarde.

Fox didn't want to wash her ears.
She said, "No, no, no… I don't want to wash my ears. No way, no!"

"They say that when you don't wash your ears, you can't hear the melodious songs of the birds!" a funny Pig said.

QUIZ	HOW DO YOU SAY:
	ears, hear, melodious, songs, funny, pig

La renarde ne voulait pas laver ses oreilles. Elle dit : « Non, non, non… Je ne veux pas laver mes oreilles. Pas question ! »

« On dit que quand on ne se lave pas les oreilles, on ne peut pas entendre les chants mélodieux des oiseaux ! » lui dit un drôle de cochon.

Pig didn't want to wash his nose.
He said, "No, no, no… I don't want to wash my nose. No way, no!"

"They say that when you don't wash your nose, you can't smell the sweetly scented flowers nor your Mummy's cakes!" a friendly Duck said.

QUIZ	HOW DO YOU SAY:
	nose, flowers, Mummy, cakes, friendly, duck

Le cochon ne voulait pas laver son nez.
Il dit : « Non, non, non… Je ne veux pas laver mon nez. Pas question ! »

« On dit que quand on ne se lave pas le nez, on ne peut pas sentir la douce odeur des fleurs, ni celle des gâteaux de ta maman ! » lui dit un sympathique canard.

Duck didn't want to wash his neck.
He said, "No, no, no… I don't want to wash my neck. No way, no!"

"They say that when you don't wash your neck, you can't turn your head anymore," a bouncing Rabbit said.

QUIZ	**HOW DO YOU SAY:**
neck, turn, head, bouncing, rabbit	

Le canard ne voulait pas laver son cou.
Il dit : « Non, non, non… Je ne veux pas laver mon cou. Pas question ! »

« On dit que quand on ne se lave pas le cou, on ne peut plus tourner la tête ! » lui dit un lapin sauteur.

Rabbit didn't want to wash his hands.
He said, "No, no, no… I don't want to wash my hands. No way, no!"

"They say that when you don't wash your hands, everything you touch becomes filthy dirty forever!" a mocking Cat said.

<table>
<tr><td>QUIZ</td><td>HOW DO YOU SAY:</td></tr>
<tr><td colspan="2">hands, everything, touch, dirty, forever, mocking, cat</td></tr>
</table>

Le lapin ne voulait pas laver ses mains.
Il dit : « Non, non, non… Je ne veux pas laver mes mains. Pas question ! »

« On dit que quand on ne se lave pas les mains, tout ce qu'on touche devient très sale pour toujours ! » lui dit un chat moqueur.

Cat didn't want to brush his teeth.
He said, "No, no, no… I don't want to brush
my teeth. No way, no!"

"They say that when you don't brush your
teeth, you will never be able to eat fruits and
sweets again!" a kind little boy said.

<table>
<tr><td>QUIZ</td><td colspan="2">HOW DO YOU SAY:</td></tr>
<tr><td colspan="3">brush, teeth, never, eat, fruits, sweets, kind, little boy</td></tr>
</table>

Le chat ne voulait pas brosser ses dents.
Il dit : « Non, non, non… Je ne veux pas
brosser mes dents. Pas question ! »

« On dit que quand on ne se brosse pas les
dents, on ne peut plus jamais manger de
fruits ou de bonbons ! » lui dit un gentil petit
garçon.

The little boy didn't want to take a bath.
He said, "No, no, no… I don't want to take a bath.
No way, no!"

"When you don't take a bath every day, you smell
really bad and your skin starts crawling with bugs,"
his super daddy explained. "It isn't nice to smell
bad and have your skin crawl with bugs, is it?"

<table>
<tr><td>QUIZ</td><td>HOW DO YOU SAY:</td></tr>
</table>

bath, every day, skin, bugs, super daddy, nice

Le petit garçon ne voulait pas prendre son bain.
Il dit : « Non, non, non… Je ne veux pas prendre
mon bain. Pas question ! »

« Quand on ne prend pas son bain tous les jours,
on sent très mauvais et notre peau est pleine de
microbes. » lui expliqua son super papa. « Ce n'est
pas agréable de sentir mauvais et d'avoir plein de
microbes sur la peau. N'est-ce pas ? »

The little boy thought a lot about it… and because he really didn't want to smell bad and have bugs crawl over his skin, he ran to the bathroom and decided to take a bath straightaway.

"You are such a good boy! You are very well behaved! I'm so proud of you!"

His daddy gave him a big kiss and a bear hug.

<table>
<tr><td>QUIZ</td><td>HOW DO YOU SAY:</td></tr>
</table>

thought, because, bathroom, take a bath, straightaway, proud

Le petit garçon y pensa très fort… et parce qu'il ne voulait vraiment pas sentir mauvais et avoir des microbes partout sur la peau, il courut vite vers la salle de bain et décida de prendre un bain aussitôt.

« Quel grand garçon ! Tu te comportes très bien ! Je suis très fier de toi ! »

Son papa lui donna un gros bisou et un énorme câlin.

THE END

FIN

ISBN 9781910909300 (PAPERBACK)
eISBN 9781910909317 (EBOOK)